Crockpot Recipes This Winter

50+ Super Easy One Pot Slow Cooker Recipes

Set 'n Forget

Copyright © 2015 Maggie Fisher

All Rights Reserved.

Table of Contents

Chicken Soup -4

Red Chili Bacon -5

Buffalo Chicken -6

Corned Beef and Cabbage -7

Pork Carnitas -8

Fajitas -9

Cabbage Rolls -10

Creamy Zucchini Soup -11

Stuffed Pepper -12

Chicken Taco -13

Crockpot Philly Cheese Steak -14

Chicken Stew -15
Spicy Broccoli Soup -16

Creamy Cauliflower and Cheddar Soup -17

Sweet and Sour Trout -18

Spicy Fish Stew -19

Garden Cabbage Soup -20

Mexican Crockpot Roast -21

Italian Meatballs -22

Minestrone Veggie Soup -23

Butter Paneer Chicken Curry -24

Turkey Stew -25

Crockpot Barbeque -26

Crockpot Chicken Curry -27

Swiss Steak -28

Lamb Stew -29

Poached White Fish Fillets -30

Crockpot Pizza -31

Crockpot Pulled Pork -32

Pork and Poblano Stew -33

Herbed Chicken Mushrooms -34

Chicken Gizzard -35

Ginger Beef Stew -36

Cheesy Crockpot Sausage Breakfast -37

Healthy Turkey Sausage Breakfast -38

Great Crock-Pot Chili Breakfast -39

Mozzarella and Pepperoni Crock Pot Pizza -40

Crock Pot Taco Soup -41

Vegetarian Crockpot Fajitas -42

Buttery Sauce with Asparagus -43

Crockpot Basil Chicken -44

Sausage with peppers Egg Bars -45

Chorizo -46

Cheese Lasagna -47

Easy Pepperoni Pepper Quiches -48

Fennel Turkey Sandwiches -49

Ham with Broccoli Bites -50

Avocado Burger Patties -51

Salami Mushroom Muffins -52

Crockpot Bacon and Egg Quiche -53

Crockpot Buttery Pumpkin with Nuts -54

Chicken Bake Crockpot Breakfast -55

Crockpot Bacon Hash -56

Winter is upon us, the holidays are already here, and we all want good, warm and comfort foods on our table. Coming home from a long day's work to find bubbling soup or creamy stew ready to be served is always delighting. Even better, waking up on a chilly morning with the wonderful aromas of breakfast casserole coming from the kitchen. ☺

A slow-cooker, or a crockpot is a perfect kitchen tool for lazy people like you and I. And here is why:

1) Minimum workload: Most of the time you just throw in the ingredients, turn on the slowcooker, and come back later to serve.

2) Zero hassle: Once you've set the crockpot, there's no need to visit it again to mix up the ingredients and stuffs like that. Set and forget. It's that simple.

3) One pot policy: Everything happens in a single pot. This eliminates the winter struggle of washing all the extra dishes.

4) Preserves nutrition: Because the food is slow cooked, the nutrients inside are not destroyed by the sudden and excessive heat.

5) Environment and Pocket friendly: Slowcookers require minimum electrical energy to operate and studies indicate that they are more energy efficient than conventional ovens.

6) Slow cooked foods are incredibly delish!

So, without further ado, let's slow cook.

~ The recipes included in this cookbook are extremely simple and easy to make. You can make them before leaving home for work in the morning, or before going to bed in the night. We hope you enjoy the warm food. If you are planning to get a slowcooker, please make sure you get the digital one. Happy winter! ~

Chicken Soup

Preparation Time: 10 min

Cook time: 6 hours

Serves: 5

Ingredients

2 Tablespoons olive oil

3 Onions, sliced

2 Green Bell Peppers, thinly sliced

7 Chicken Thighs (Boneless)

3 Slices of Bacon

2 teaspoons turmeric

2 Tablespoons Minced Garlic

2 tablespoons Minced Ginger

3 Tablespoons Lemon Juice

1/4 Cup Chopped Cilantro

1 Cup Chicken Stock

3 Tablespoons Tomato Paste

1 Green Onion

Salt and Pepper to taste

Directions

Pour the oil in the Crockpot.

Slice the onions. Uniformly distribute the slices throughout the bottom of the pot.

Repeat the same for the bell peppers.

Place the boneless chicken thighs in the pot.

Distribute the slices of bacon all over the chicken.

Add the seasonings-turmeric, salt, pepper, minced garlic, minced ginger. Stir well.

Pour lemon juice and chicken stock, followed by the tomato paste.

Cook the soup on low settings low for 6 hours or until the meat becomes tender.

When the soup is done, garnish it with cilantro and green onions.

Add cheese toppings and serve it warm.

Red Chili Bacon

Preparation Time: 15 min
Cook time: 6 hours
Serves: 5

Ingredients

2 Tablespoons Olive Oil

5 Thickly cut bite-sized Bacon

1 Pound (450gm) Pork, finely chopped

3 large Onions, chopped

3 tomatoes, diced

2 Green Bell Pepper, sliced

2 Tablespoon Tomato Paste

1 Pack Chili Seasoning

Salt, Pepper to taste

Directions

Pour the olive oil in your Crockpot.

Place the chopped onion and bell pepper in the Crockpot.

Add finely chopped ground pork.

Start seasoning the meat with salt, pepper, onion & garlic powder. Add the chili seasoning as per your taste.

Cut bacon into small pieces. Cook, drain, cool and put it in the Crockpot.

Dice the tomatoes and add them into the Crockpot.

Pour the tomato paste.

Cook for 6 hours on low settings.

Buffalo Chicken

Preparation Time: 7 min

Cook time: 7 hours

Serves: 6

Ingredients

2 Tablespoons Olive oil

6 Chicken Breasts

2 tablespoons Hot sauce

½ Cup Tomato Sauce

½ Chicken Stock

1 Tablespoon Ranch Dressing

Chopped Parsley/Cilantro

Salt and pepper to taste

Directions

Pour olive oil in the Crockpot.

Place the chicken in the Crockpot.

Pour the tomato sauce over the chicken followed by the hot sauce and chicken stock.

Pour the ranch dressing on top.

Season with salt and pepper.

Cook the chicken on low setting for 7 hours.

When done, shred the chicken into fine pieces using forks.

Add chopped parsley/cilantro on top and serve it warm.

Corned Beef with Cabbage

Preparation Time: 20 min

Cook time: 7 hours

Serves: 8

Ingredients

2 tablespoons Olive Oil

2 packages, thinly sliced Corned Beef (600gm/1.3 pound each)

1 Cabbage, medium sized

2 Large Onions, finely diced

4 garlic cloves, crushed

2.5 Cups Water

½ teaspoon Ground Coriander

½ teaspoon Ground Mustard

½ teaspoon Black Pepper

½ teaspoon Ground Thyme

Salt and pepper to taste

Directions

Pour the olive oil in your Crockpot.

Add the diced onion.

Add 2½ cups of water.

Season with all the spices.

Add the mixture of the spices on both sides of the beef and place it on top.

Cover the Crockpot and cook on low settings for 6 hours.

Now the cabbage. Toss out the outermost layer of cabbage and shred the remaining.

Place the shredded cabbage in the Crockpot and cook for an additional 1 hour on medium setting.

Serve it warm.

Pork Carnitas

Preparation Time: 15 min
Cook Time: 8 hours
Serves: 8

Ingredients

2 Tablespoons Olive Oil

2.5 Pound (1.3kg) Pork shoulder, lean

2 large Onions, sliced

4 Garlic Cloves, minced

1 Tablespoon Cumin

2 Tablespoon Thyme

½ teaspoon Chili Powder

½ cup of Water

Salt and Pepper to taste

Directions

Pour the oil in the Crockpot.

Slice an onion and put the pieces in the Crockpot.

Sprinkle the minced garlic over the onions.

Drain out the excessive fat from the meat.

Season both sides of the pork with the mixture of Thyme, Cumin, Salt, Pepper, Chili powder.

Spread the remaining mixtures of spices in the Crockpot.

Place the meat into Crockpot.

Add ½ cup of water.

Cook for 6-8 hours on low settings until the pork is fork tender and easily shreds.

Fajitas

Preparation Time: 10 min
Cook Time: 7 hours
Serves: 6

Ingredients

1 tablespoon Olive Oil

1.5 pound Beef Stew

2 large Onions, diced

2 Green Bell Peppers, sliced

5 Garlic cloves, chopped

2 Tablespoon Chili powder

½ cup tomato paste

½ tablespoon Oregano

Salt and pepper to taste

Directions

Pour olive oil in the Crockpot.

Add onion and capsicum in the pot.

Mix the spices together and put into the Crockpot.

Season the stew with salt, pepper and spices and add the stew in the Crockpot.

Cook for 6-8 hours on low settings until the meat is pull-apart tender.

Drain out excessive liquid.

If necessary, season with more salt and pepper.

Serve it warm.

Cabbage Rolls

Preparation Time: 10 min
Cook Time: 6 hours
Serves: 5

Ingredients

10 Cabbage leaves, large

1 Pound Ground beef

1 beaten egg

1 cup cooked rice

1 cup hard, granular Cheese

4 Garlic Cloves, minced

1 tablespoon Onion powder

½ Cup Tomato sauce

1 tablespoon lemon juice

1 bunch of fresh, finely chopped Parsley

Salt and pepper to taste

Directions

Boil the Cabbage leaves on the stove for 4 minutes.

Pour ½ cup tomato sauce into the Crockpot.

In a bowl, mix up the all ingredients – egg, cheese, garlic, onion powder and pepper.

Add ground beef and cooked rice in the mixture and stir it so that the meat is seasoned well.

When the cabbage leaves are cooled, measure about one-fourth cup of the beef- mixture and spread on the bottom of each cabbage.

Bring sides of leaf together and roll it up.

Place the cabbage roll(s) into the Crockpot.

Pour the lemon juice on the rolls

Cook on medium setting for 6 hours.

Garnish with chopped Parsley and serve warm.

Creamy Zucchini Soup

Preparation Time: 5 min
Cook Time: 6 hours
Serves: 6

Ingredients

2 Tablespoon Olive Oil

2 large Onions, chopped

3 tomatoes, diced

1 cup celery, chopped

2 green bell peppers, sliced

1 tablespoon minced ginger

3 cups Vegetable Broth

3 medium Zucchini

½ teaspoon Salt

1 teaspoon Pepper

½ teaspoon black pepper

1 teaspoon dried oregano

1 teaspoon dried basil

2 Tablespoons Whipped Cream

Directions

Pour oil in the Crockpot.

Add the chopped onion. ginger, celery, diced tomatoes, bell peppers.

Pour the vegetable broth in the Crockpot, then add the Zucchini pieces.

Combine salt, pepper, black pepper, oregano, basil and pour in the Crockpot. Stir well.

Cook for 6 hours on low setting until the zucchini becomes tender.

When cooked, use an immersion blender and blend it in the Crockpot itself.

Add the whipped cream on top and stir.

Serve it warm.

Stuffed Bell Pepper

Preparation Time: 7 min

Cook Time: 7 hours

Serves: 4

Ingredients

5 large Green Bell Peppers

1 pound Ground Beef (450g)

1 cup cooked rice (optional)

1 Cabbage, small, shredded

2 medium onions, chopped

3 cloves garlic, minced

½ Cup Tomato sauce, spicy

1 Cup Cheese, shredded

½ teaspoon Salt

½ teaspoon Pepper

1 Cup Vegetable stock

Directions

Take a medium bowl and mix all the stuffing ingredients; beef, rice, cabbage, onions, garlic, sauce, cheese, salt and pepper. Mix until well combined.

Cut the top of bell pepper off and discard all the seeds.

Stuff all the capsicums with the stuffing.

Fill up your Crockpot with 1 cup of vegetable stock.

Place the stuffed bell pepper in your Crockpot.

Cook for 7 hours under low settings.

Top with some cheese and serve it warm.

Chicken Taco

Preparation Time: 5 min
Cook Time: 5 hours
Serves: 4

Ingredients

2 teaspoons Olive Oil

1 cup Chicken Broth

2.2 Pound (1 kg) Chicken Breast, boneless

2 Tablespoons Lemon juice

½ teaspoon salt

½ teaspoon pepper

1 small bunch fresh Cilantro, finely chopped

½ cup Swiss Cheese

Directions

Pour the olive oil in the Crockpot.

Add the chicken broth and chicken breast. Season them with salt and pepper.

Stir the mixture.

Cook for 5 hours under low settings.

Once cooked, drain the meat and shred it using two forks.

Pour the lemon juice and stir again.

Garnish with cilantro.

Add Swiss cheese on top.

Serve it warm.

Philly Cheese Steak

Preparation Time: 15 min
Cook Time: 7 hours
Serves: 4

Ingredients

2 Tablespoon Olive Oil

1 pound (450g) round Steak, thinly sliced

1 Green Bell Pepper large, thinly sliced

1 cup Mushroom, fresh, sliced

2 Onions, medium sized, sliced

1 cup Beef Broth

3 Garlic Cloves, minced

½ teaspoon Pepper

½ teaspoon Salt

6 slices of Provolone Cheese

Marinara Sauce

Toasted Roll / Buns

Directions

Pour the olive oil in the Crockpot.

Season the steak with pepper, salt and place it in the Crockpot.

Add onion, capsicum and minced garlic in the pot.

Stir the mixture.

Pour in the broth and cook for 7 hours under low settings until the meat becomes tender.

Drain the meat and slice it.

Fry the meat with some veggies and butter until it is slightly brown.

Toast the bread/roll until crusty.

Stick a slice of cheese on each side of the roll.

Using tongs put the meat and veggies and pile on top of rolls.

Use Marinara sauce as topping.

Serve it warm.

Chicken Stew

Preparation Time: 7 minutes
Cook time: 6 hours
Serves: 6

Ingredients

1 Tablespoon Olive Oil

1 ½ cup russet potatoes, skin peeled, medium slices

1 cup carrot, medium slices

1 pound (450g) Chicken breasts, cubed and fried (until golden)

½ cup onions, chopped

2 Garlic Cloves, minced

½ cup Sour Cream

1 can chicken soup

½ teaspoon garlic powder

Salt and pepper to taste

Directions

Pour in the oil.

Place the veggies on the bottom of the crockpot.

Sprinkle the seasonings evenly over the veggies.

Add the chicken and pour in the soup.

Cook for 6 hours under low heat settings.

Spicy Broccoli Soup

Preparation Time: 8 minutes
Cook Time: 6 hours
Serves: 8

Ingredients

4 cups Broccoli florets

1 tablespoon Olive oil

½ cup Onions, chopped

2 teaspoons Ginger, minced

3 Garlic cloves, chopped

2 roasted Green Bell Peppers

2 cups vegetable stock

2 cups water

½ cup sour cream

Salt and pepper to taste

Directions

Heat the olive oil in a frying pan.

Add onion and garlic. Quick fry for 2 minutes.

Transfer the mixture in your Crockpot.

Add broccoli florets, bell peppers, vegetable stock and water. Stir well.

Season with salt and pepper.

Cook for 6 hours under low settings.

When done, puree the soup with an immersion blender.

Stir in the sour cream.

Serve it warm.

Creamy Cauliflower and Cheddar Soup

Preparation Time: 7 minutes
Cook Time: 6 hours
Serves: 6

Ingredients

2 tablespoons melted butter

4 cups Cauliflower florets

¼ cup all purpose flour

1 cup milk

1 cup Vegetable Stock

1 cup water

½ cup Onion, chopped

2 Garlic cloves, minced

1 teaspoon salt

1 teaspoon pepper

½ cup heavy Cream

½ cup grated Cheddar

½ cup shredded Parmesan

Directions

Heat the butter in a frying pan.

Add onion and garlic. Cook until tender.

Stir in the flour and cook for 2 minutes, stirring constantly.

Now stir in milk until smooth.

Transfer the mixture in your Crockpot.

Add cauliflower florets in the pot. Stir well.

Pour the vegetable stock followed by water.

Season the mixture with salt and pepper.

Cook for 6 hours under low settings.

When done, pour in the heavy cream.

Puree the soup with a blender.

Top with grated cheese.

Serve it warm.

Sweet and Sour Trout

Preparation Time: 7 min
Time: 5 hours
Serves: 4

Ingredients

2 tablespoons Olive oil

4 Trout Fillets

2 teaspoons Soy Sauce

1 teaspoon grated Ginger

1 tablespoon sugar

1 cup Marinara Tomato Sauce

1 tablespoon Lemon juice

Salt and Pepper to taste

Directions

Pour the oil in your Crockpot.

Place the trout fillets.

Add soy sauce, ginger, and sugar over it.

Season with salt and pepper.

Add the tomato sauce.

Cook for 5 hours under low settings.

Serve it warm.

Spicy Fish Stew

Preparation Time: 5 min
Cook time: 6 hours
Serves: 6

Ingredients

4 White Fish Fillets

2 small potatoes, quartered and sliced

1 medium carrot, quartered and sliced

1 cup Green Onion, chopped

2 Green Bell Peppers, sliced

1 cup Tomato Sauce

½ cup Hot Sauce

2 cups Vegetable Stock

1 teaspoon garlic paste

1 teaspoon turmeric

1 teaspoon salt

1 bunch fresh parsley, to garnish

Directions

Place the sliced potatoes on the bottom of your crockpot.

Add all the remaining ingredients.

Cook for 6 hours under low settings.

Garnish with freshly cut parsley and serve warm.

Garden Cabbage Soup

Preparation Time: 10 min
Cook Time: 5 hours
Serves: 4

Ingredients

4 cups cabbage, shredded

2 Green Onions, chopped

1 cup Vegetable Stock

2 stalks Celery, sliced

3 Garlic Cloves, chopped

2 medium Tomatoes, diced

1 teaspoon thyme, dried

½ teaspoon Cardamom powder

1 bunch Cilantro, small

1 cup water

Salt and pepper to taste

Directions

Mix together cabbage, onion, celery, garlic and tomatoes in your Crockpot.

Pour vegetable stock and water in the pot.

Season the mixture with salt and pepper.

Add the cardamom powder and dried thyme. Stir well.

Cook for 5 hours under low settings.

When done, add freshly cut cilantro on top.

Serve it warm.

Mexican Crockpot Roast

Preparation Time: 10 min
Cook Time: 8 hours
Serves: 6

Ingredients

1 Tablespoon Olive Oil
2 pound Beef chuck roast, boneless
3 cloves Garlic, minced
1 teaspoon Thyme, minced
1 teaspoon Rosemary, dried
½ teaspoon Cumin powder
1 teaspoon Chili Powder
½ cup Hot Sauce
2 Tablespoons Lemon Juice
Salt and Pepper to taste

Directions

Take a bowl and mix the olive oil, garlic, thyme, rosemary, cumin, salt, pepper and lemon juice.

Apply this mixture over all faces of the meat and rub well.

Place the beef in your Crockpot.

Cook for 8 hours under low settings until the meat becomes fork-tender.

Serve warm.

Italian Meatballs

Preparation Time: 15 min

Cook Time: 7 hours

Serves: 6

Ingredients

2 pounds ground meat (beef/pork)

1 egg

1 cup Parmesan Cheese, finely grated

1 cup Tomato Sauce

1 cup shallot, chopped

½ cup breadcrumbs, dried

1 teaspoon dried Basil

1 teaspoon dried Parsley

1 teaspoon dried Oregano

1 teaspoon garlic powder

2 teaspoons Italian seasoning

½ cup Beef Stock

¼ cup red wine

Salt and pepper to taste

Directions

Take a bowl and beat the egg with salt and all the seasonings.

Add the chopped shallot, ground meat, breadcrumbs and the cheese. Mix well.

When done, take some portion of the mixture and roll it into a shape just a little bigger than a golf ball size.

Place these balls into the crockpot.

In the same bow, mix the tomato sauce, wine, stock and pour all over the meatballs.

Cook for 6-7 hours under low settings or until the meatballs are no longer pink in the middle.

Minestrone Veggie Soup

Preparation Time: 10 min
Cook time: 8 hours
Serves: 6

Ingredients

2 Green onions, chopped

1 cup tomatoes, diced

2 carrots, chopped

1 cup potato chopped

3 cloves Garlic, minced

2 cups Broccoli, chopped

2 cups Cauliflower, chopped

1 cup Mushroom, sliced

2 cups Vegetable Stock

3 stalks Celery, sliced and chopped

¼ cup fresh Parsley, chopped

1 cup tomato juice

½ cup Parmesan Cheese, grated

3 cups water

1 tablespoon Italian Seasoning

2 bay leaves

Salt and Pepper to taste

Directions

Add all the veggies (onion, tomato, carrot, potato, garlic, broccoli, cauliflower, mushroom, celery, parsley) in the Crockpot. Add bay leaves and sprinkle the seasonings on top.

Pour vegetable stock, tomato juice and water in the Crockpot. The level of liquid should be just above the top of the Veggies.

Cook for 8 hours or until the veggies become tender.

When done, puree about a cup of veggies by using immersion blender.

Pour the puree back and mix it up so it gives a thick texture to the soup.

Add grated cheese on top and serve it warm.

Butter Paneer Chicken Curry

Preparation Time: 10 min
Cook Time: 5 hours
Serves: 4

Ingredients

4 Chicken Thighs, boneless

5 oz. Paneer packet

½ cup Tomatoes, finely crushed

3 tablespoons Butter

1 tablespoon Olive Oil

3 cloves of Garlic, chopped

1 teaspoon curry powder

½ teaspoon chili flake

5 sprigs Cilantro, chopped

1 cup water

Salt and pepper to taste

Directions

Season the meat with olive oil (rub on the meat), salt and pepper.

Slice the Paneer into pieces put it aside.

Pour the butter in the Crockpot.

Add garlic and crushed tomato, sliced Paneer, followed by a cup of water.

Now place the chicken in the Crockpot. Add curry powder and chili flake. Mix well.

Cook for 4 hours under low settings.

When done, garnish with cilantro.

Serve it warm.

Turkey Stew

Preparation Time: 5 min
Cook Time: 8 hours
Serves: 4

Ingredients

2 tablespoons olive oil

4 Turkey thighs, boneless

1 Cup raw Cabbage, shredded

1 Onion, small, chopped

1 stalk celery, chopped

2 garlic cloves, chopped

1 pound button mushrooms

½ or 1 cup turkey stock, depending on required thickness of texture

½ cup chopped cilantro

1 tablespoon Turkey seasoning

4 cups water

½ teaspoon black pepper

¼ teaspoon cayenne pepper

Salt and pepper, to taste

Directions

Pour the Olive Oil in your Crockpot.

Add onion on top of it followed by cabbage and celery.

Place all the remaining ingredients, except cilantro. Add the seasonings.

Cook for 9 hours under low settings.

Use cilantro to garnish.

Serve it warm.

Crockpot Barbeque

Preparation Time: 10 min
Cook Time: 8 hours
Serves: 4

Ingredients

2 tablespoons olive oil

2 medium onions, sliced

2 lbs beef meet, boneless

3 cloves of garlic, minced

½ cup barbeque sauce

Salt and Pepper to taste

Directions

Season the beef with salt and pepper.

Heat a frying pan and pour the oil.

Quick fry the onions and garlic until light brown.

Transfer the mixture in your Crockpot.

Add the beef meat, barbeque sauce and stir.

Cook for 8 hours under low settings.

Serve it warm.

Crockpot Chicken Curry

Preparation Time: 10 min
Cook Time: 8 hours
Serves: 6

Ingredients

2 Tablespoons Olive Oil

1.3 lbs Chicken, minced

½ cup tomato puree

1 tablespoon lemon juice

1 teaspoon ginger, shredded

4 mint leaves

2 tablespoons curry powder

½ Green Chili, chopped

Directions

Quick-fry the chicken in a frying pan with tomato puree, ginger, mint leaves, salt, and peppers.

Transfer the ingredients in your Crockpot.

Cook for 9 hours under low settings.

Add the lemon juice on top.

Serve it warm.

Crockpot Swiss Steak

Preparation Time: 10 min

Cook Time: 8 hours

Serves: 4

Ingredients

2 Tablespoons Olive Oil

1 lbs Steak, boneless

½ cup flour

2 potatoes, peeled and quartered

1 cup tomato, diced

½ cup Beef Stock

3/4 can cream of Mushroom soup

2 onions, sliced

2 carrots, sliced

1 Green Bell pepper, thinly sliced

2 minced garlic cloves

½ cup tomato sauce

4-5 sprig cilantro, chopped

Directions

Coat the steak with flour. Then season the steak with salt and pepper. Set aside.

Brown the meat with oil in a skillet and drain.

Place sliced potatoes, carrots, onions, bell pepper, garlic at the bottom of the crockpot.

Transfer the steak on top of your Crockpot. Sprinkle salt as per your taste.

Add all the remaining ingredients; tomato, tomato sauce, beef stock, mushroom soup over the meat.

Cook for 8 hours under low settings.

Garnish with some chopped cilantro.

Serve it warm.

Lamb Stew

Preparation Time: 15 min
Cook Time: 7 hours
Serves: 4

Ingredients

2 tablespoons Olive Oil

2 pound lamb stewing meat, boneless, trimmed

¼ cup flour, all purpose

1 cup potato, diced

1 cup baby carrots

1 onion, chopped

½ teaspoon dried Thyme

2 Green Bell Peppers, diced

2 garlic cloves, chopped

2 tomatoes, sliced

½ cup Beef Stock

1 cup water

1 bay leaf

1 cup Marinara sauce

4-5 sprig Parsley

Salt and pepper to taste

Directions

Season the meat with salt and pepper. When done, coat with flour.

Heat a frying pan over medium flame. Pour the oil and add the seasoned lamb. Fry it for 5 minutes or until golden brown.

Transfer the meat in your Crockpot.

In the same pan, cook the onion, bell pepper for a couple of minutes or until tender. When done, transfer into the crockpot.

Now add potatoes, carrot, thyme, garlic, tomatoes, sauce. Stir well.

Pour the beef stock, water and add the bay leaf.

Season well with salt and pepper (remember, the meat is already seasoned)

Cook the meat for 8 hours under low settings.

Chop the parsley and add over the meat.

Serve it warm.

Poached White Fish Fillets

Preparation Time: 10 min
Cook Time: 6 hours
Serves: 4

Ingredients

4 white fish fillets
1 cup coconut milk
4-5 sprig Cilantro, chopped
1 bay leaf
1 scallion, chopped
Salt and pepper to taste

Directions

Heat the coconut milk to a simmer on a stovetop.

Pour the milk into the Crockpot.

Place fish fillets in the Crockpot. Add all the ingredients except cilantro.

Season well with salt and pepper.

Cook for 6 hours under low settings.

Top with the chopped cilantro and serve warm.

Crockpot Pizza

Preparation Time: 10 min
Cook Time: 4 hours
Serves: 4

Ingredients

2 lbs Chicken, grounded

2 cups shredded part-skim mozzarella cheese

2 cups shredded cheddar cheese

1 cup mushrooms, sliced, drained

½ teaspoon onion powder

½ teaspoon garlic powder

1 teaspoon dried basil

Directions

Blend the grounded chicken, mozzarella cheese and the cheddar cheese together.

Transfer them into your Crockpot.

Add the sliced mushrooms, onion and garlic powder, basil and mix well.

Flat the upper face.

Cook for 5 hours under low settings.

Serve it warm.

Crockpot Pulled Pork

Preparation Time: 10 min
Cook Time: 8 hours
Serves: 6

Ingredients

2 Tablespoons Olive Oil

2 lbs Pork Loin, trimmed

1 cup onion, chopped

½ teaspoon ginger paste

2 cloves garlic, chopped and minced

2 Tablespoons lemon juice

1 cup coconut milk

1 teaspoon black pepper

1 tablespoon apple cider vinegar

Salt and pepper to taste

Directions

Trim down the excess fat from the pork. Using a knife, slice a crisscross pattern on top of the meat so that it can render.

Take a small bowl and add the olive oil, ginger paste, minced garlic, lemon juice, black pepper, vinegar, salt and pepper.

Stir the mixture until it forms a paste. Apply the paste all over the meat.

Add the chopped onion in your Crockpot.

Place your seasoned meat over it.

Pour the cup of coconut milk.

Cook for 8 hours under low settings.

When done, shred the pork with 2 forks.

Serve it warm.

Pork and Poblano Stew

Preparation Time: 10 min

Cook Time: 8 hours

Serves: 4

Ingredients

3 Poblano chili peppers, charred and sliced

1 lb pork shoulder, trimmed, cubed

2 Tablespoons Olive oil

½ cup Onion, chopped

2 garlic cloves, minced

1 teaspoon Cumin

1 Tablespoon dried Oregano

1 cup chicken stock

½ cup sour cream

4-5 sprigs cilantro, chopped

Directions

Char the Poblano chili on all sides. When done, remove the seeds inside. Thinly slice the peppers.

Pour the oil in a frying pan. Place the pork and fry until light brown.

Transfer the meat into your Crockpot.

Add all the ingredients and season well with salt and pepper.

Cook for 8 hours under low settings.

When done, pour the sour cream on top with the chopped cilantro.

Serve it warm.

Herbed Chicken Mushrooms

Preparation Time: 15 min
Cook Time: 8 hours
Serves: 6

Ingredients

6 Chicken thighs, boneless
1 pound assorted mushrooms, sliced
½ cup onion, sliced
1 cup vegetable broth
½ teaspoon basil, dried
3 cloves garlic, minced
1 teaspoon Thyme
3-4 sprig Parsley, chopped
Salt and Pepper to taste

Directions

In a bowl combine all the sliced mushrooms, onion, vegetable broth, basil, garlic, thyme and parsley. Stir well.

Place the chicken thighs into your Crockpot

Add the mixture of ingredients on the top.

Season well with salt and pepper.

Cook for 8 hours under low settings.

Serve it warm.

Chicken Gizzard

Preparation Time: 5 min
Cook Time: 7 hours
Serves: 4

Ingredients

1.5 lbs Chicken Gizzards

1 cup onion, chopped

1 cup baby carrots, chopped

1 cup celery, chopped

3 cloves garlic, minced

¼ cup tomato paste

½ cup red wine

1 cup chicken broth

½ cup water

5-6 sprigs cilantro, chopped

Salt and pepper to taste

Directions

Place all the ingredients in your Crockpot except cilantro.

Stir well. The meat should be partially submerged in the mixture of water, paste and wine.

Season well with salt and pepper.

Cook for 7 hours under low settings.

When done, sprinkle the cilantro on top.

Serve it warm.

Ginger Beef Stew

Preparation Time: 5 min
Cook Time: 7 hours
Serves: 4

Ingredients

2 Tablespoons Olive Oil

1 lb beef meat, cubed

1 Green Bell Pepper, sliced

1 cup tomato, diced

1 cup green onion, chopped

1 cup beef stock

4 cloves garlic, minced

½ teaspoon black pepper

1 tablespoon ginger, grated

½ cup Marinara sauce

½ teaspoon Sesame seeds

Directions

Pour the olive oil in a frying pan and fry the beef meat until light brown.

Add the bell pepper, onion, and garlic and quick fry for 2 more minutes.

Transfer the mixture into your Crockpot.

Add all the remaining ingredients; tomato, black pepper, beef stock, ginger, marinara sauce, salt and pepper.

Cook for 9 hours under low settings.

Serve it warm.

Cheesy Sausage Breakfast

Preparation Time: 10 minutes
Cook Time: 8 hours
Serves: 6

Ingredients

1.5 cups of Sausage Crumbles

1½ teaspoon of garlic paste

1 cup of sun dried tomatoes cut into slices

¼ cup of basil leaves

½ cup of Parmesan cheese

½ cup of Ricotta cheese

5 eggs

1 cup milk

2 scallion, finely chopped

Salt and pepper to taste

Olive oil

Directions

Spray the Crockpot vessel with olive oil and keep aside.

Take a large bowl, and add all the ingredients one by one and mix well.

Pour this mix into the Crockpot and set the timer for 8 hours and at low temperature.

Serve.

Healthy Turkey Sausage Breakfast

Preparation Time: 15 minutes

Cook Time: 8 hours

Serves: 4

Ingredients

3 cups of chopped turkey

1 cup of cream cheese

6 eggs, beaten well

½ cup of small broccoli flowerets

½ cup onion, finely chopped

½ cup bell pepper, sliced

2 cups of milk

1 teaspoon of thyme

2 tablespoons of mustard sauce

1 cup of tomato puree

1 cup of chicken stock

Directions

Spray the Crockpot vessel with cooking oil and keep aside.

Pour 2 tablespoons of oil in your skillet and heat it. Once hot, add the onion, bell pepper, turkey sausages and slow fry the mixture for 10 minutes. Keep aside.

Take a large bowl, and add all the other remaining ingredients one by one and mix well. Add the sausage mix and also stir well.

Pour this mix into the Crockpot and set the timer for 8 hours and at low temperature.

Great Chili Breakfast

Preparation Time: 15 minutes

Cook Time: 8 hours

Serves: 4

Ingredients

1.5 lbs of ground beef

1.5 lbs of ground pork

¼ cup of chopped parsley

½ cup onion, chopped

1 cup of tomato puree

1 cup of stewed tomato with Mexican seasoning (optional)

3 cloves of garlic minced

2 celery sticks chopped finely

4 tablespoons of cayenne powder

Salt to taste

2 bay leaves

1 teaspoon of black pepper powder + 1 teaspoon of oregano powder+ 2 teaspoon of roasted cumin powder

Directions

Spray the Crock-Pot vessel with cooking oil and keep aside.

Take a large skillet, spray with cooking oil, and once hot add the ground beef and the pork and stir on high heat. Cook for 10 minutes under high flame until the meat has absorbed its juices and also become a bit brown.

Take a large bowl, and add all the ingredients one by one and mix well. Add the meat mix also at this point.

Pour this mix into the Crockpot and set the timer for 8 hours and at low temperature and scoop and serve the next morning for breakfast.

Mozzarella and Pepperoni Crockpot Pizza

Preparation Time: 15 minutes

Cook Time: 7 hours

Serves: 4

Ingredients

½ cup of mushrooms cut into cubes

½ cup of green peppers, sliced

4 oz of pepperoni cut into pieces

½ cup of pizza sauce (tomato sauce is fine)

½ cup of parmesan cheese grated

½ cup of mozzarella cheese grated

4 black olives, sliced

6 eggs

¼ cup almond milk

Salt and pepper to taste

2 teaspoons of oregano

Directions

Spray the Crockpot vessel with cooking oil and keep aside.

Beat the eggs well, add milk, and then add the mushrooms, red peppers, green peppers, pepperoni, sat and the pepper and the oregano and stir well.

Pour this mix into the Crockpot and finally top with pizza sauce, the two cheeses, and sliced olives.

Now set the timer to the lowest temperature and let it cook for about 7 hours.

Cut into wedges and serve hot.

Crockpot Taco Soup

Preparation Time: 15 minutes
Cook Time: 8 hours
Serves: 6

Ingredients

1 lb shredded chicken

1 cup pinto beans

1 cup kidney beans

1 cup niblet corn

1 cup tomatoes, diced

½ cup chopped celery

½ cup tomato paste

2 cups chicken stock

2-3 green chilies, chopped

3 tablespoons taco seasoning

Salt and Pepper, to taste

Directions

Cook, drain and shred the meat.

Add all the ingredients to the crockpot.

Stir well and cook on low for 8 hours.

Garnish with sour cream.

Veggie Crockpot Fajitas

Preparation Time: 10 minutes

Cook Time: 6 hours

Serves: 5

Ingredients

10 flax/flour tortillas

2 tablespoons olive oil

1 red pepper, finely cut

1 green pepper, finely cut

2 onions, finely cut

1 cup cherry tomatoes, halved

½ teaspoon of chili flakes

½ teaspoon of roasted cumin powder

1 cup of finely sliced cabbage

½ teaspoon of garlic salt

2 tablespoons of lemon juice

2 tablespoons of sesame paste

Directions

Spray the Crockpot vessel with cooking oil and keep aside.

Take a large bowl, and add the peppers, onions, tomatoes, cabbage, chili flakes, cumin powder, garlic salt and 2 tablespoons of olive oil and mix well.

Set the timer at a low temperature and add all the vegetable mix and cook for 6 hours.

When cooked, warm the tortillas, and add spoonful of the cooked vegetable mix and sprinkle and bit of lemon juice and sesame paste and a bit of olive oil and munch into a moist delectable vegetable fajita.

Buttery Sauce with Asparagus

Preparation Time: 15 minutes
Cook Time: 6 hours
Serves: 5

Ingredients

2 pounds of asparagus spears

5 tablespoons of salted butter

½ cup of fresh cream

1 tablespoon of all purpose flour

¼ cup of milk

1 bacon slice cut into bits

1 teaspoon of chicken bouillon

Pepper to taste

Directions

Spray the Crockpot vessel with cooking oil and keep aside.

Mix the flour in the milk and then add the chicken bouillon and ensure that is well dissolved.

Beat the cream, add the pepper and add this mix into the milk.

Now melt butter and pour into the Crockpot. Wash and clean the asparagus spears and place on top of the melted butter. Mix well.

Next, add the coconut flour milk mix, cream mix, almond slices, and bacon bits and stir well.

Cook at low temperature for about 6 hours until the asparagus is cooked, moist and buttery.

Basil Chicken

Preparation Time: 15 minutes

Cook Time: 8 hours

Serves: 6

Ingredients

2 lb. of boneless chicken breasts cut into fine cubes

Handful of basil leaves

1 cup of spinach leaves

Handful of coriander leaves

½ cup of celery sticks finely chopped

2 garlic cloves, chopped

2 cups of chicken stock

1 cup of mushrooms cut into cubes

1 large onion, chopped

Salt and pepper to taste

Directions

Spray the Crockpot vessel with cooking oil and keep aside.

Take a blender and place the basil, coriander leaves, spinach, garlic, salt and pepper and blend to a fine puree.

Pour this puree into a large bowl, add the chicken, celery sticks, chicken stock, mushrooms, onion and mix well.

Place the mixed ingredients into the Crockpot and then cook for about 8 hours at the lowest temperature. It will have to cook in its on juices and the final product will be dark green moist chicken along with gravy.

Scoop this mix into some fresh lettuce leaves. Serve hot!

Sausage with Peppers Egg Bars

Preparation Time: 15 minutes

Cook Time: 7 hours

Serves: 5

Ingredients

12 oz of Italian sausages chopped into smaller pieces

2 green peppers, sliced

½ cup onion, sliced

5 eggs, well beaten

1 cup tomato, diced

1 cup of kale leaves

Salt and pepper to taste

1 cup of milk (regular/coconut/almond)

4 tablespoons of butter

Directions

Spray the Crockpot vessel with cooking oil and keep aside.

Take a frying pan and fry the sausages until light brown and keep aside.

Now take a large bowl, add the beaten eggs, peppers, onions, tomatoes, kale leaves, salt, pepper and milk and stir well.

Put 2 tablespoons of butter in Crockpot, and then pour half of the egg mix.

Now, place the sausages carefully on the watery egg mix. After that, pour the remaining egg mix and add the rest of the butter on top.

Close the pot and cook on low for about 7 hours until eggs are firm and are ready to come off the edges.

Cut into bars and serve with some mustard sauce.

Chorizo breakfast

Preparation Time: 35 minutes
Cook Time: 8 hours
Serves: 8

Ingredients

2 cups of mushrooms sliced

2 cups diced potato

½ cup black beans

½ cup pinto beans

¼ cup of parsley

10 oz of pork chorizo

1 medium onion, diced

1 tablespoon of minced garlic

4 eggs (optional)

5 oz. cream cheese

2 cups milk (or chicken stock for a different taste)

½ cup of parmesan cheese grated

2 teaspoons of pepper powder

Directions

Spray the Crockpot vessel with cooking oil and keep aside.

Take a large frying pan, pour a tablespoon of olive oil and fry the onion until caramelized. Keep aside.

In the same pan, add more oil, add the chorizo, garlic and sauté for a couple of minutes. Finally toss in the parsley and the mushrooms and sauté for another couple of minutes until the veggies get tender. When done, keep aside.

Now in a bowl, add the rest of the ingredients and mix the chorizo and onions into this mix. Pour into Crockpot and cook at low temperature for 8-9 hours until everything is tender and light brown at the edges.

Cheese Lasagna

Preparation Time: 10 minutes

Cook Time: 7 hours

Serves: 8

Ingredients

1 lb lean ground beef

1 package lasagna noodles (12 oz)

1 onion, chopped

2 cups of mozzarella cheese grated (reserve some for topping)

½ cup grated parmesan

1 cup of tomato sauce

½ cup tomato paste

1 teaspoon dried oregano

1 teaspoon of garlic powder

Salt and pepper to taste

Directions

Spray the Crockpot vessel with cooking oil and keep aside.

Take a large frying pan, add a bit of oil and brown the meat along with the garlic powder and chopped onion. Add the tomato sauce, tomato paste, salt, pepper and oregano. Mix well and cook until heated through. Keep aside.

Mix together the mozzarella and grated parmesan in a separate bowl.

Put the meat mixture onto the bottom of the crockpot. Then add the uncooked lasagna noodle on top of it. If needed, break the noodles so the fit in the crockpot.

When done, add in the layer of cheese mixture on top.

Cook under low heat settings for 6-7 hours.

Easy Pepperoni Pepper Quiches

Preparation Time: 10 minutes

Cook Time: 8 hours

Serves: 4

Ingredients

1 pepper, sliced

8 pepperoni slices

4 eggs

3 tablespoons of flax seed powder

1 onion chopped finely

1 teaspoon of garlic powder

1 cup milk

1 cup of Parmesan cheese

½ cup of tomato sauce

Salt and pepper to taste

Directions

Spray the Crockpot vessel with cooking oil and keep aside.

Take a large bowl, add the eggs, flax seed powder, peppers, pepperoni, onion, garlic powder, milk, cheese, salt and pepper and mix well

Pour this mixture into the Crockpot and drop spoonful of tomato sauce on top of the mix.

Cook at low temperature for about 8 hours (or overnight) and your Quiche will be ready in the morning.

Fennel Turkey Sandwiches

Preparation Time: 10 minutes

Cook Time: 8 hours

Serves: 4

Ingredients

1 pound of turkey mince

4 eggs

1 cup of cream cheese beaten well

1 teaspoon of fennel seed powder

1 teaspoon of mustard powder

½ cup of milk

1 teaspoon of garlic powder

1 onion sliced thin+ ½ cup of crushed walnuts

Salt and pepper to taste

4-6 lettuce leaves

Directions

Spray the Crockpot vessel with cooking oil and keep aside.

Take a large bowl, and add the turkey mince, eggs, fennel seed powder, mustard powder, milk, garlic powder, salt and pepper and combine well.

Place this mix in the Crockpot and top with sliced onions, and beaten cream cheese. Then add the crushed walnuts on top of the onions.

Finally close the Crockpot and set the timer for about 8 hours (overnight) and keep at the lowest temperature.

In the morning, scoop out the well cooked meat and place in each lettuce leaves, add a bit of mayonnaise or tomato sauce and enjoy warm!

Ham with Broccoli Bites

Preparation Time: 15 minutes

Cook Time: 7 hours

Serves: 10

Ingredients

2.5 pounds of ham cleaned and chopped

2 cups of gruyere cheese grated

2 cups broccoli flowerets

Salt and pepper to taste

2 teaspoons of thyme

2 cups of almond milk

1 cup of chicken stock

8 large eggs beaten well

Directions

Open the Crockpot and place all the ingredients in it and mix well.

Set the timer for 7 hours and let it cook over night.

In the morning, cut into squares and serve warm.

Avocado Burger Patties

Preparation Time: 20 minutes

Cook Time: 6 hours

Serves: 6

Ingredients

2.5 cups of mashed avocado

4 eggs

5 tablespoons regular flour

2 pounds of hamburger meat

1 teaspoon of chili flakes

½ cup soy sauce

1 cup of grated papaya

Salt and pepper

½ cup of melted butter + ½ cup milk mixed together

Directions

Grease the Crockpot and keep aside.

Place the avocadoes, 2 eggs, flour, salt and mix well. Divide into 12 small patties.

In another bowl, place the hamburger meat, soy sauce, chili flakes, papaya, salt and pepper and 2 eggs and combine well. Make 6 patties out of the meat mix.

Now place one meat patty in between 2 avocado patties. Like that you will get 6 avocado burger patties.

Place these patties in the Crockpot and slowly pour the butter and milk mixture little by little. Do not directly on top if the patty but through the small gaps.

Set time for 6 hours (overnight) and cook at the lowest temperature possible.

Salami Mushroom Muffins

Preparation Time: 20 minutes

Cook Time: 6 hours

Serves: 6

Ingredients

6 slices of salami sliced

1 cup of chopped Portobello mushrooms

½ cup onions, chopped

¼ cup green pepper

¼ cup red pepper

2 cups of milk

6 eggs

3 basil leaves

1 cup of baby spinach

½ cup of Parmesan cheese

Salt to taste

Directions

Grease the Crockpot and keep aside.

Place the ingredients into one large bowl and mix well.

Put the mixture into the Crockpot, and heat under low settings for 6 hours.

Cut out as you like, serve them hot with some sour cream.

Bacon and Egg Quiche

Preparation Time: 20 minutes
Cook Time: 5 hours
Serves: 4

Ingredients

5 slices of bacon fried and chopped

8 eggs

2 cups of milk

½ cup of melted butter

Pepper to taste

1 cup of cottage cheese crumbled

½ cup of green scallions

Directions

Grease the Crockpot and keep aside.

Pour the milk into the Crockpot. Then slowly break each egg into the milk. Be careful not to break the yolk.

Then sprinkle the fried bacon, cheese, pepper, scallions and finally spoon the butter over them.

Cook at a low temperature for about 5 hours, until you get a well - cooked and firm quiche.

Buttery Pumpkin

Preparation Time: 10 minutes

Cook Time: 6 hours

Serves: 4

Ingredients

1 cup of pumpkin puree

100 grams of melted butter

2 cups of milk

½ cup of maple syrup (or 2-4 tablespoons sugar)

4 eggs

2 tablespoons of almonds, walnuts and pecans each, lightly crushed

Directions

Grease the Crockpot and keep aside.

Now, add the ingredients in a bowl and mix well.

Pour into Crockpot and cook at low temperature for 5-6 hours until set.

Scoop this rich maple infused pumpkin dish and enjoy.

Chicken Bake Breakfast

Preparation time: 10 min
Cook Time: 6 hours
Serves: 4

Ingredients

2 tablespoons olive oil

4 chicken breasts, quartered

2 garlic cloves, chopped

1 cup onion, diced

1 cup carrot, diced

1 cup canned tomato

¼ cup basil leaves

2 tablespoons red wine vinegar

Directions

Get a frying pan and pour the olive oil. Heat it and add the chicken breasts. Cook well until golden brown.

When cooked, add the chicken in the Crockpot. Add the garlic, tomato, onion, carrot and basil.

Mix well and drizzle the red wine vinegar.

Cook the meat on low settings for 6 hours.

Serve warm.

Bacon Hash

Preparation time: 10 min
Cook Time: 7 hours
Serves: 6

Ingredients

8 bacon slices, coarsely chopped

1 large onion, diced

4 cups sliced mushrooms

2 potatoes, peeled and halved

2 large carrots, peeled and halved

1 tablespoon grain mustard

4-5 cups broth

2 tablespoons olive oil

1 pinch chili flakes

Salt and Pepper

Directions

Combine all the ingredients in your Crockpot.

Cook for 7 hours under low settings.

Garnish with chopped cilantro and serve the hash warm.

Made in the USA
Middletown, DE
22 August 2016